ELDAR SAMADOV

D0543948

TERROR: EVENTS, FACTS, EVIDENCE

LONDON, 2015

Preface

This book is based on research carried out since 1988 on territorial claims of Armenia against Azerbaijan, which led to the escalation of the conflict over Nagorno-Karabakh. This escalation included acts of terror by Armenian terrorist and other armed gangs not only in areas where intensive armed confrontations took place but also away from the fighting zones. This book, not for the first time, reflects upon the results of numerous acts of premeditated murder, robbery, armed attack and other crimes through collected material related to criminal cases which have been opened at various stages following such crimes. The book is meant for political scientists, historians, lawyers, diplomats and a broader audience.

HERTFORDSHIRE PRESS

Published in United Kindom
Hertfordshire Press Ltd © 2015
Suite 125, 43 Bedford Street
Covent Garden, London
WC2E 9HA

e-mail: publisher@hertfordshirepress.com
www.hertfordshirepress.com

Terror: Events, Facts, Evidence
© Eldar Samadov

Senior adviser: Eldar Mahmudov
Adviser: Khanlar Valiyev
Editor: Rauf Mammadov
Translator: Shahla Babayeva
Editor: Charles Van Der Leeuw

*Published by the support of the Embassy
of the Republic of Azerbaijan in London*

*British Library Catalogue in Publication Data
A catalogue record for this book is available from the British Library
Library of Congress in Publication Data
A catalogue record for this book has been requested*

ISBN: 978-1-910886-00-7

Foreword

In this century, as human beings we see ourselves as part of an advanced society, with accomplishments of many fields that have not been witnessed in the history of civilization. Yet, in the area of humanity, we have been observers of brutality on levels that many find incomprehensible. In some cases, people have been massacred to obtain territory; while in others, they have been systematically tortured, raped, and murdered in order to obliterate a genetic group or race. Some of these cruel and uncivilized actions have been brought to the attention of the world and those who perpetrated the actions brought to trial and to justice. However, in other cases, the world at large is unaware of the events and those who are responsible have not had to answer for their atrocious actions.

One such case has occurred in Azerbaijan. A decree of the President of the Republic of Azerbaijan, dated on March 1, 2001 assigned an important task. A State Commission was established to collect the legal and historical documents relating to terrorism, genocide, and ethnic cleansing carried out against Azerbaijanis by Armenia. The role of the State Commission was to systematise this information, and to present it for the recognition to the world community.

"Terror: Events, Facts, Evidences" relates and documents evidence, not just of one specific attack, but of systemic events going back to the beginning of the twentieth century. These events not only involve kidnapping, torture, and killing of men, women, children and the elderly who were part of the civilization population, they involve massive destruction. Settlements, as well as industrial, agricultural and other enterprises have been obliterated, along with water and hydraulic engineering infrastructure. Dwellings and residential areas with hospitals and medical clinics and transportation and communications no longer exist. The estimated economic damage is in the billions of dollars.

Because it happened more recently, one of the best documented cases can be made about the town of Khojaly. On the night of February 25-26, 1992, the Armenian armed forces with support of the infantry guards regiment No. 366 of the former Soviet Union seized the town.

"As a result, 613 persons were killed, including 106 women, 63 children and 70 elderly people, 1.275 peaceful inhabitants were taken hostage, while the fate of 150 persons remains unknown to this day. In the course of the tragedy 487 inhabitants of Khojaly were severely maimed, 8 families were completely wiped out , 25 children lost both parents, and 130 children one of their parents."

The purpose of the attack was to create a second Armenian State on the territory of the Republic of Azerbaijan.

I cannot overstate the importance of this publication. If the human race is to survive and mankind advance, we must document and bring to light all cases of such injustice. Not only is this important to honour the memory of those who have been slaughtered, it is important to help the world recognize a better way for the future.

— *Professor Nabil Ayad*
Director, The Academy of Diplomacy
and International Governance
Loughborough University in London

Introduction

The Republic of Azerbaijan is one of the most dynamically developing countries in the Southern Caucasus. But as the XX Century drew to a close, Azerbaijan had been the victim of aggression by the neighbouring Republic of Armenia ever since 1988.

As a result of it, one-fifth of Azerbaijan's national territory had come under occupation, more than 20,000 people had been killed, andd more than 50,000 people permanently injured and invalid. For more than 25 years, over a million people have been living as refugees on their own country's territory. Known among humanitarian organisations as Internally Displaced Persons (IDP), these victims of ethnic cleansing operations, which accompanied the acts of genocide against the Azeris, have been deprived of all basic human rights.1)

Also as a result of the occupation, 900 settlements have been looted, burnt and razed. 6,000 Industrial, agricultural and other enterprises have been annihilated. Over 150,000 residential buildings, over 9,000 square metre of residential areas, 4,366 social and cultural buildings including 695 medical centres and clinics have been destroyed. Throughout the occupied territories, agricultural land, water and other technical infrastructure and means of transportation and communication have been lain waste. In all, the damage caused by the aggression campaign has been estimated at more than 300 billion US dollar. 2)

On the occupied territories 927 libraries, 464 historical monuments and museums, more than 100 archeological sites and other invaluables have been ruined. From museums, over 40,000 artifacts and other objects, including unique exibits, have been stolen. 3) Thus, from the regional historic museum of Kelbajar ancient rugs were taken to Armenia as well

1

as objects from the Shusha branch of the National Museum of Azerbaijan, while the unique Bread Museum of Agdam and the stone age artifact museum of Zenguilan were completely destroyed. The value in cash of these cultural and historic assets is impossible to determine. By plundering Azerbaijan's resources in this manner, the Republic of Armenia has violated the provisions in the Convention of The Hague regarding protection of cultural property during armed conflicts and in the Paris Convention regarding illegal trafficking of cultural property.

Due to its military aggression, its support of terrorism, the state of Armenia has been kept outside political and economic projects meant to contribute to the prosperity and development of states successfully carried out in the region. As a result, large parts of the population have been forced to leave the country due to extreme economic hardship.

Having suffered from Armenian terrorism, the Republic of Azerbaijan nevertheless remains in favour of international coordination in order to reach a peaceful settlement of the problem, in accordance with international and other interstate agreements. In the struggle against terrorism, Azerbaijan has intensified its cooperation with foreign countries and their relevant security services. Azerbaijan has been among the very first states to join the anti-terror coalition in the wake of the tragedy of September 11 2001 in the USA.

Armenian terrorism has been among the protagonists of international terrorism, with an experience of over a hundred years. The term "Armenian terrorism" was first introduced in 1982 in a report by Andrew Corsun under the header "Armenian terrorism: a Profile" (US Department of State Bulletin no. 82, Washington D.C., August 1982 pp. 31-35). 4) The publication followed a series of terrorist attacks in Lebanon along with terrorist attacks on US military engaged in humanitarian work in emergency zones.

The history of Armenian terrorism in the form of organised crime goes back to the late XIX Century. Organised and systematic terrorist activities by Armenians took off with the establishment of the movement Armenakan in the eastern-Turkish city of Van in 1885, followed by the foundation of the Hynchak movement in Geneva, Switzerland, in 1887 and the Dashnaksutyun (also known as Dashnak or Armenian Revolutionary Federation or ARF) in Tbilisi in 1890. Established as political parties, the main aim of these movements was the creation of a "Greater Armenia" through acts of violence and terror. In fact, violence and aggression had already been an integral part of Armenian elites' ethnic psychology and ideology for centuries.

The first act of terrorism in the modern sense of the word by Armenians was the attack on the Moscow Underground on January 8 1977, accompanied by the demand to attach the Azeri regions of Nakhchivan and Nagorno-Karabakh to Armenia. In the explosion of a device on a crowded Underground train between the stations Ismailovskaya and Pervomaiskaya 7 people were killed and 32 seriously injured. Three Armenian terrorists were to be found guilty of committing the crime. Hakop Stepanian, Stepan Zatikian and Zaven Bagdasarian were sentenced by the Supreme Court of the USSR to death by a firing squad. 5)

The first time Armenian terrorists used hostage-taking as a method was the occupation of the Ottoman Bank in 1896, carried out by 26 activists of the ARF, who put political demands forward as a condition to release the staff held at gunpoint. 6)

In October 1919, the ARF held its 9th General Assembly in Yerevan, where it decided to launch a fresh terror offensive under the code name Nemesis after the Greek goddess of heavenly retaliation. The aim of the campaign was to take revenge on those held responsible for the "Armenian genocide" of 1916 within the Ottoman empire and the alleged massacre of Armenian citizens in Baku in 1918.

The list included 650 persons, including the leaders of the Ottoman empire and the Democratic Republic of Azerbaijan, and including 41 top-level priority targets. A special fund and a supervising committee chaired by the Armenian Ambassador to the United States Armen Garo were established. Kracha Papazian was appointed chief information officer under the guise of a Turkish student. Units of 3 to 5 members were formed to track the targets and carry out their killings. Isolated targets were killed by a single sniper and those who went around with bodyguards by a hit squad of two or three members.

As coordination centres the offices of two Armenian newspapers, Cakatamart in Istanbul and Droshak in Boston were used. As part of the Operation Nemesis the following officials were killed during the 1920s:

Tbilisi, June 19 1920: Fatali Khankhoisky, former Prime Minister of the Democratic Republic of Azerbaijan (former DRA politician Khalilbey Aghayev was injured in the attack);

Hasanbey Aghayev, former vice-speaker of the Parliament of Azerbaijan;

Berlin, March 15 1921: Talat Pasha, former interior minister and chairman of the Ottoman empire;

Rome, December 5 1921: Said Halim Pasha, former chairman of the Ottoman empire (among the culprits was former Armenian ambassador to Rome Mikhail Vartanian);

Berlin, April 7 1922: Djemal Azmi, former governor of Trabzon;

Berlin, April 17 1922: Gehaddin Shakir, founder of the Tashkilaty Makhsusa;

Istanbul, July 18 1921: Behbudkhan Djavanshir;

Tbilisi, July 25 1922: Djemal Pasha, former navy minister of the Ottoman empire.

Apart from former state officials, the terrorist cells targeted and killed a number of Armenians in Istanbul who were accused of having collaborated with the Turkish authorities during the 1916 events.

As for the 1918 events in Baku, it is good to have a look at what happened there and in other parts of Azerbaijan at the time. 7) In March 1918, Russia's Bolshevik leader Vladimir Lenin appointed Stepan Shaumian as "special commissioner for the Caucasus" and dispatched him to Baku. Meant as vehicles to seize power in Baku, the Bolsheviks created paramilitary units, operating under cover, consisting of Armenian Dashnaks. On March 31 1918, a massacre of Azeri citizens in the city began, carried out, according to later declarations made by Shaumian, by 6,000 armed troops under the Baku Council and 3,000 to 4,000 men in arms consisting of Dashnak activists. 8)

The onslaught lasted three days, during which Armenian terror units supported by the Bolsheviks carried out surprise attacks on residential neighbourhoods inhabited by Azeris, killing everyone. In the city of Baku alone, between March 30 and April 1 12,000 Azeris were killed and the rest of them forced to flee. 9) A German witness of the events by the name of Kulner was to describe what he swa in 1925 as follows: "Armenians dashed into Azeri Muslim districts and killed everybody, cutting them to pieces with swords and piercing them with bayonets. After several days of onslaught, 87 corpses of Azeris were found in a mound with their ears and noses cut off, their bellies torn open, their private parts slashed. The Armenians showed no mercy, not even on children and elderly." 10)

In the aftermath through the month of April altogether 50,000 non-combatant citizens of Azerbaijan were massacred, murdered and removed from their premises by force. Locations included Baku, Shemaka, Guba, Lenkoran, Mughan and other areas. In all, during the two major extermination operations held in the Southern Caucasus in the early XX Century (1905-1907, 1918-1920) some 100,000 people have been murdered. 11)

Investigations following the March mass murders in Baku also revealed the find, in one of Baku's neighbourhoods, of 57 dead bodies of women with their ears and noses cut off and their bellies torn open, materials of the Investigation Commission were to show. 12)

An American agronomist named Leonard Ramsden Hartwill wrote a book, Ovanes Apresian, after the latter's memoirs. Apresian was a commanding Armenian activist who had taken part in the massacres of Azeris in the province of Yerevan as well as in Sharur, Dereleyez, Surmeli, Kars and other regions. Hartwill notes that in Baku, Armenians killed 25,000 Azeris with the help of Russians and Britons. 13)

As noted, extermination operations by Dashnak forces were not limited to Baku, but also took place in Shemakha, Goba, Yerevan, Zanguezour, Karabakh, Nakhchivan, the Iranian cities Urmiya, Khoy and Salmas and the Turkish cities of Erzurum and Kars. In Van in the year 1915 alone, some 30,000 Muslim Turks were murdered and survivors driven from their homes by force by Armenian terror squads. From the Aegean Sea to the eastern Caucasus, some 2.5 million Muslims, most of them ethnic Turks, were killed. 15)

In March and April 1918, 8,027 unarmed citizens of Shemakha were killed, and many cultural monuments including the Djuma mosque burnt and razed, the Commission's documents show. 16)

In the Djavanshir Gaza (= province) and the Djebrayil Gaza 28 and 17 villages respectively were burnt to the ground and their population exterminated on April 29 1918. Some 3,000 Azeri survivors, mostly women, children and elderly people who had taken refuge near Gumru were encircled and slaughtered. 17)

In the province of Nakhchivan,, Armenian armed forces burnt several villages, while in the province of Zanguezour 115 Azeri villages were destroyed and 3,257 men, 2,276 women and 1,296 children were murdered in the process. 18) In all, according to the Commission's investigation results, in this particular region 10,068 Azeris were killed or permanently mutilated, along with 135,000 Azeris living in the province of Yerevan where 199 villages were destroyed. 19) At a later stage, armed Armenian forces moved into Karabakh, where between 1918 and 1920 150 villages were destroyed and their populations massacred. 20)

A new dimension to the modern history of global terrorism was given in 1975 with the founding of the Armenian Secret Army for the Liberation of Armenia (ASALA) with the main aim to establish a Greater Armenia, stretching over parts of eastern Turkey and northern Iran and including Nagorno-Karabakh and Nakhchivan. ASALA's main targets were Turkish diplomats. Within years, 110 terrorist acts were carried out on 38 locations in 21 different countries in which 42 Turkish and 15 foreign diplomats were murdered. Among the most spectacular attacks was the one on Ankara's Esenboga Airport, in which nine people were killed and 72 injured. 21)

Following the collapse of the Soviet Union, Armenia gained independence and started to support terrorism on official state levels, including terrorism as an integral part of its policy of aggression. Stockpiles of forensic evidence gathered during investigations demonstrate that terrorist acts against the civil population of Azerbaijan, including car bombs and explosives on board public transport, have been carried out by special forces of Armenia, financed by the Armenian government.

In the eary 1990s, official institutions in Armenia started a campaign for the rehabilitation of activists of the Dashnaksutyun, ASALA, MAG, Armenian Unity, the Armenian Liberation Front and other terrorist organisations, giving them accommodation, financial resources and other necessities for them to continue their activities.

Official Armenia also started collecting signatures for the release of Varujan Garabedian, the man who had carried out the terrorist attack on Orly Airport near Paris on July 15 1983. As a result of the attack, eight people had been killed and 60 injured. In 2000, he was released on a French court order and found refuge and official protection in Armenia.

Monte Melkonian, a popular terrorist in Armenia, had been sentenced on November 28 1985 by a French court to six years in prison. After his release in 1990, Melkonian who was born in the US state of California came to Armenia and joined the Armenian forces in Nagorno-Karabakh where he used his experience as a terrorist abroad. Monte Melkonian was the commander of a terror squad during the attack on and subsequent occupation of the Khodjavend district in Azerbaijan, as shown in the book My Brother's Road written by his brother Markar and published in New York in 2005. 22) Monte Melkonian was killed in Nagorno-Karabakh in 1993 and buried in Yerevan. Armenia's President Levon Ter-Petrossian attended the funeral. He was declared national hero of Armenia and a detachment of the defence ministry charge with underground operations was named after him.

One other popular terrorist by the name of Grant Marekarian has been a member of the terrorist group Dro, subordinate to the Dashkansutyun party, and a key figure in the supply of arms from Armenia to terrorist groups active in Nagorno-Karabakh. 23)

Vazgen Sislian, who had organised the attack on the Turkish embassy in Paris in 1981, was awarded the title of hero of the Karabakh war by the Armenian President Robert Kocharian for his participation in acts of terror against Azeri citizens. 24)

Two terrorists from the Middle East, one of whom was nicknamed Abu Ali (a Lebanese nickname for a torturer/executor) and the other was named Hilbert Minasian stood under special protection of Armenia's state intelligence services while carrying out massacres among unarmed Azeri citizens. 25)

On the night of February 25/26 1992, one of the gravest crimes in human history was committed, known as the tragedy of Khodjaly. With the aim to complete the creation of an Armenian state on the territory of Azerbaijan, Armenian forces with the support of the former Soviet infantry regiment no. 366 seized the town of Khodjaly in Nagorno-Karabakh.

The majority of children and elderly were killed inside their homes. In the cold winter night many civilians were forced to come out of their homes and were killed in the streets, while some managed to escape into the mountains and the forests, where they were hunted down and slaughtered as well. Civilians were shot and mistreated by the Armenians. Captives and hostages taken by the Armenians were tortured and kept under inhuman conditions, humiliated and insulted – all in violation of international human rights.

As a result, 613 persons were killed, including 106 women, 63 children and 70 elderly, while 1,275 unarmed inhabitants were taken hostage. The fate of 150 persons was to remain unknown forever. In the course of the tragedy 487 inhabitants of Khodjaly were severely mutilated, 8 families were completely wiped out, 25 children lost both their parents and 130 children one of their parents.

The State Committee of the Republic of Azerbaijan for prisoners of war, hostages and missing people registered 185 missing citizens of Azerbaijan.

The number of 95 Azeri citizens remaining in captivity indefinitely as part of the 185 missing persons included 11 children among whom were two girls, and 23 women among whom 11 were elderly.

In the course of investigations in connections with the Khodjaly mass murder during the preparation of this book evidence was produced that Seyran Oganian, defence minister of the Republic of Armenia and commander of the 366th Regiment, as well as Valery Chitchian, along with more than 50 officers and privates serving in the regiment took part in the attack.

According to information gathered by the Human Rights Watch centre Memorial, 200 corpses were brought in from Khodjaly to Agdam within four days, where signs of tens of different kinds of maltreatment and humiliation were noted on their bodies. Forensic investigations were made on the corpses of 130 men and 51 women. It appeared that 151 persons had died of bullet wounds, 20 by hand grenades' fragments, while 10 persons had been killed with blades. The medical centre also discovered a man who had been scalped alive. 26)

The act of genocide in Khodjaly is only one example out of a large number of criminal acts in the course of the Armenian aggression against Azeris by Armenian terror groups.

The war of terror against Azerbaijan had become consistent during the 1980s as Armenian terrorist organisations operating in various countries around the world received financial and organisational from Armenia and the Armenian diaspora.

During the occupation of Nagorno-Karabakh and seven surrounding districts, Armenian special brigades were deployed not just in areas of military operations but also in settlements where non-combatant citizens lived, with the aim to create mass panic by inflicting heavy losses of human lives, spread terror as a result of which hundreds of people were killed.

According to a decree of the President of Azerbaijan dated March 1 2001, the State Committee for Prisoners of War, Hostages and Missing Persons was re-staffed, with the task to collect historic and legal documents regarding terrorism, genocide and ethnic cleansing by Armenians against Azeris in order to provide a systematic database to be presented to the world community.

The decision was made to submit material to the General Prosecutor's office of the Republic of Azerbaijan in connection with crimes committed by Armenian armed units and terrorist groups. Humiliation of captured military personnel belonging to the Azeri armed forces in Nagorno-Karabakh as well as of other persons protected by international human rights, subjecting them to torture, brutal treatment, personal humiliation, rape, regular beating, incitement to suicide or otherwise driving to persons' deaths and causing harm to their health, committed by Armenian armed forces, were included in the Criminal Code of the Republic of Azerbaijan, in particular in Article 100 section 1 (victimising abusing material and other dependence of a person by brutal methods, humiliation of personal dignity with the aim incite a person to suicide or make him inclined to kill himself), Article 108 section 2 (systematic beating and other acts of torture), Article 109 section 4 (rape in particular of juveniles and carried out by a dangerous recidivist) in accordance with Article 115 section 3 (violation of laws and rules of war). The first criminal case in this context, no. 0340, was filed by the Prosecutor General of the Republic of Azerbaijan as of November 27 2002.

The same criminal case was assigned to the serious crimes investigation department under the Military Prosecutor's Office of the Republic of Azerbaijan on November 29 2002. By a decision taken on December 6 2002, a joint task force was established consisting of staff members of the General Prosecutor, the Military Prosecutor and the Ministry of National Security of the Republic of Azerbaijan.

Subsequent investigations demonstrated the need to extend the legal domain involving the criminal case from attacks on single persons (prisoners of war, hostages) to violations of human rights such as genocide, forcibly modifying the constitutional order, forming illegal armed units, mass murder, expulsion of people from their native lands, large-scale acts of terror, blowing up civil and administrative buildings and environmental crimes.

Subsequently, on December 18 2003 a joint decree by the Prosecutor General's office, the Ministry of Internal Affairs and the Ministry of National Security of the Republic of Azerbaijan was signed to establish a joint investigation team in connection with research into crimes committed by separatist forces of Nagorno-Karabakh and Armenian regular armed forces.

Since 1988, the Prosecutor General's office, the Ministry of Internal Affairs and the Ministry of National Security of the Republic of Azerbaijan have carried out investigations into more than 600 criminal cases in which citizens of Azerbaijan who were forced to leave Nagorno-Karabakh and other occupied territories were victims of robbery of their property, cultural and historic monuments were destroyed, prisoners of war and hostages were tortured, mutilated and killed, along with sabotage, terrorism and other serious crimes committed by Armenian armed forces.

A decision made on December 30 1999, which came into force as of September 1 2000, determined criminal liability in accordance with Article 214 of the Criminal Code in cases of threatening public safety, creating panic among the population, murder with the aim to influence decisions and their acceptance by state authorities or international organisations, inflicting serious damage on property, spreading social unrest causing social outbreaks, arson and other acts with the same goals.

Before the legislative adaptions as of September 2001, terrorism as such was not defined in the Criminal Code of Azerbaijan and acts resorting under it had been falling under Article 61 (sabotage), Article 70 (banditry), Article 94 (premeditated murder under aggravating conditions). Subsequently, Article 59 (acts of terrorism) which came into force as of September 1 2000 put criminal liability on attempts on the lives or inflicting grave physical injuries of public figures and of representatives of foreign states. Prior to this, criminal liability was provided by Article 277, still in vigour (attempt on the life of a state or other public authority/act of terrorism) according to which terrorism includes an attempt on the life of a public figure or representative of a foreign state committed with the aim to discontinue the target's political activity or service or take revenge for events related to them.

Acts of terror committed by Armenian terrorist groups in Nagorno-Karabakh and adjacent areas

Criminal case no. 38 related to the explosion of a car on the bridge across the river Khalfalichay

On October 7 1989 around 21.30hrs, a car bomb blew up the motorway bridge across the river Khalfalichay on the southern outskirts of the town of Khankendi, followed by the opening of criminal case no. 38 by an investigative team of the USSR KGB for violation of article 61 of the all-Union Criminal Code (sabotage). Khankendi had been the residence of the Khans of Karabakh till the end of the XVIII Century and means "city of the Khan". On July 7 1923, after the consolidation of Soviet power, the Autonomous Province of Nagorno-Karabakh was established with Khankendi as its administrative centre. Later, the town was renamed Stepanakert after Stepan Shaumian. In 1991, the National Assembly of the Republic of Azerbaijan changed the name back into Khankendi due to what it saw as "historic injustice".

The explosion stood not in itself and was soon to be followed by several other bomb attacks on motorways in various parts of Nagorno-Karabakh which took place in 1989 and 1990 and were included in the overall investigation supervised by P. A. Sokolov, senior inspector on serious cases within the investigation department of the KGB.

On the night of 13/14 November 1989 around 1.05 a.m. on the 6th kilometre mark on the crossroad between the motorways Yevlakh-Lachin and Khankendi (Stepanakert)-Shusha a roadside bomb went off. On November, criminal case no. 14 was opened by the prosecutor of the Autonomous Province of Nagorno-Karabakh based on article 61 of the Criminal Code (sabotage) of the Republic of Azerbaijan.

On February 18 1990 around 8.25hrs a.m. a coach of the type Ikarus 250/59 with state number plate 34-67AQ1 moving from Yevlakh to Shusha near the 105 kilometre mark on the Yevlakh-Lachin motorway was blown up by unknown persons, causing severe loss of human life. The same day, in accordance with article 61 of the Criminal Code (sabotage) of the Republic of Azerbaijan, criminal case no. 102004 was opened by an investigation group of the all-Union Prosecutor's office of the USSR.

As of May 14 1990, criminal cases nos. 14 and 102004 were combined into a single proceeding as the the culprits had not been identified, and on June 8 1990 the case was closed without results.

On June 24 1991, though, paramilitary forces detained a certain A. A. Abramian for an administrative offence, who in his statement declared that he had been among the perpetrators who had blown up the bridge over the river Khalfalichay, and that he was ready to provide evidence on the criminal acts' details.

The very next day, the case had been sent to a special investigation task force on the Autonomous Province of Nagorno-Karabakh to be studied by A. I. Mashin, inspector of the Azeri Prosecutor General's special investigation team for priority cases.

On September 11 1991, the team's chief inspector R. Musayev received the combined case files, re-numbered 38/33063, for further proceedings.

Criminal case no. 33028, meanwhile, revealed the name of Samuel A. Babaian, who was to be exchange the following year against Azeri hostages upon which he became "defence minister" of the self-styled Republic of Nagorno-Karabakh which he kept from 1993 to 1999 when he was arrested for the murder of the "Republic"'s "President", in connection with the blast in October 1989.

On January 4 1992 R. Mansurov, chief inspector of the department for investigations at the Ministry of National Security, filed charges against S. A. Babaian, A. A. Abramian and others in relation to criminal case no. 38/33063 which included the car bomb explosion on October 9 1980, the car blast that blew up the bridge over the river Khalfalichay on 25 October 1989, the blast on the crossroad on November 14 1989, and the later one on February 18 1990. By the time charges were filed, the case had come to include 38 different case investigations supervised by S. D. Bayramov, senior inspector of the department for high-priority investigations at the Ministry of National Security of the Republic of Azerbaijan.

On January 10 1992, criminal case no. 38 had been included in the proceedings by S. D. Bayramov based on Article 209 section 3 (non-identification of perpetrators of crimes) and the case was closed without issue.

Criminal case no. 44/33013 related to an armed attack by Armenian armed forces on a road convoy at kilometre mark 93 on the motorway Istisu-Barda

On July 11 1990 at 18.00hrs at kilometre mark 93 on the road from Istisu to Barda near the village of Hanavan in the district of Khodjav-end, an armed attack was launched on a road convoy, escorted by troops and carrying people and goods to the town of Khelbadjar. The district of Khodjavend had been created by law nr. 279-xii on November 26 1991 following the abolishment of the Autonomous Province of Nagorno-Karabakh by the Republic of Azerbaijan and comprised the former districts of Martuni and Hadrut. It was to be occupied by Armenian armed forces on October 2 1992. The attack was carried out by Zaven Vartanovich Iskhanian, Borik Vazgenovich Isgendarian, Arkadiy Abramovich Ayrian and other members of the Armenian armed forces. In the act of terrorism, three people were killed: private of military unit no. 5436 Sergey Viktorovich Mezentsev, and militiamen Shahlar Avaz Shukurov and Chimnaz Shamshir Ismailov, while 23 others were injured. On July 12 1990, a criminal case was opened based on Article 94 section 2 to 4 (premeditated murder under aggravating conditions; in force until September 1, 2000) of the Criminal Code of the Republic of Azerbaijan by the former prosecutor's office of the district of the Mardakert district in the Republic of Azerbaijan.

Following the identification of identical perpetrators, a number of criminal cases involving A. A.. Ayrian and a number of other Armenians were combined into a single criminal case. Accusations included premeditated murder, robbery and violation of equal ethnic, religious and racial rights. In charge of the proceedings was R. T. Mansurov, chief inspector of the investigations department at the Ministry of National Security of the Republic of Azerbaijan.

On July 10 1992, A. A. Ayrian was found guilty on all charges by the Supreme Court and sentenced to death. Regarding the other suspects of the crime, no identifications or information on their whereabouts became available, upon which R. T. Mansurov, chief inspector of the investigations department at the Ministry of National Security of the Republic of Azerbaijan, declared the case closed.

That decision, though, was to be revoked on February 25 2003, as the files, meanwhile updated, were sent back to the Prosecutor General's office's department of serious crimes for the investigations to be continued.

On March 3 2003, inspector A. G. Hamidov of the Prosecutor General's office's department of serious crimes for the investigations accepted the files for further proceedings. The district of Agdara had been established on August 8 1930. On September 30 1939 it was renamed Cerabert, later Mardakert, only to receive its original name back in 1990. Starting in 1990, with the aim to have the Autonomous Province of Nagorno-Karabakh handed over from Azerbaijan to the Republic of Armenia, the operations of an armed group outside the margins of the laws of the Republic of Azerbaijan conducted by Zaven Vartanovich Iskhanian and Borik Vazgenovich Isgendarian, committing assaults, premeditated murders and other crimes mentioned earlier, caused a massive exodus of people who had lived in the area for many generations.

Based on these criminal acts, a decision to file charges was made on March 28 2003, citing Article 279 section 3 of the Criminal Code (creation of armed formations or groups outside the legislation of the Republic of Azerbaijan aimed at the annihilation of human life and other destructive goals). A search warrant was issued on March 29 2003, ordering legal action against anyone violating Article 53 section 1 subsection 3 (deliberate obstruction of the course of justice and judicial investigations) of the Criminal Code of the Republic of Azerbaijan.

On May 19 2003, an arrest warrant was issued with the request to Interpol to put the names of Zaven Vartanovich Iskhanian and Borik Vazgenovich Isgendarian on the international search list.

Criminal case no. 29187 related to the bomb explosion on the passenger bus Tbilisi-Agdam

On August 10 1990, a passenger coach moving on the road from Tbilisi to Agdam was blown up in which 17 people were killed and 18 injured. Based on Article 61 (sabotage) of the Criminal Code of the Republic of Azerbaijan investigations were initiated by R. Samadov, prosecutor of the district of Khanlar. The perpetrators of the terrorist act were apprehended while preparing a second attack on the same coach line on June 17 1991.

On May 27 1992, the Supreme Court of the Republic of Azerbaijan sentenced A. Ovanesian to death by a firing squad and his fellow-perpetrator M. Tatevossian to 15 years imprisonment.

Criminal case no. 68 related to the bomb explosion at the broadcasting centre of Khankendi

On September 15 1990, Armenian terrorists blew up the broadcasting station of the Autonomous Province of Nagorno-Karabakh, located at the crossroad between Lenin Avenue and Atarbekov Street in Khankendi. The same day, based on Article 61 (sabotage) of the Criminal Code of the Republic of Azerbaijan, Khankendi district prosecutor B. A. Melkumov opened a criminal case, investigations into which were in the hands of A. V. Shemelyov, senior inspector for priority cases regarding the Autonomous Province of Nagorno-Karabakh of the KGB.

On January 21 1992, proceedings which had been placed in the hands of R. T. Mansurov, chief inspector of the investigations department at the Ministry of National Security of the Republic of Azerbaijan, were suspended for failure to identify the crime's perpetrators.

Criminal case no. 18/35208-91 related to the find of a large arms storage in the village of Dudukchu in the district of Hadrut

By a decision made on April 19 1991 by B. S. Mammadov, inspector of the Azeri Prosecutor General's special investigation team for priority cases, a criminal case was filed against A. L. Grigorian, J. R. Oganian and others based on Article 70 (banditry) as well as Article 220 section 1 (theft of firearms, explosives and ammunition; in force as of February 1 2000) of the Criminal Code of the Republic of Azerbaijan, under case number 18/32847.

Investigations revealed that on November 15 1990 at 6.00hrs a.m. two submachine guns, three hand machine guns, three rifles, one hand rifle, one revolver, two portable grenade launchers, 10 grenade shells, four submachine gun trunks, more than 1,000 submachine gun and rifle bullets of calibres 7.62 and 5.45, three units of explosives, three radio communication units, three signal rockets, three food packages, one car number plate (42-46ADC), and various military uniforms were taken from a storage. The investigations led to the detention of Manvel Sektorovich Grigorian, Valerik Telnovich Muradian, Armen Geverkovich Sayadian, Artash Tagikovich Epremian, Sarkis Cholokovich Akopian and others.

The group of detainees was first brought to the Fizuli district but the same day they were transferred to Khankendi. In accordance with Article 256 (violation of the passport regime) of the Russian Soviet Republic, General-Major V. I. Safonov, commander of the Autonomous Region of Nagorno-Karabakh convicted them to 30 days in prison, after the expiry of which they were to be released. There is no doubt that the lenience of the conviction was due to the support of separatism by Armenian and other officials and showed tolerance towards Armenian terrorist groups. On December 18 and 20, in accordance with Article 220 section 1 of the Criminal Code of the Republic of Azerbaijan, orders had been given for the preventive detention of Manvel Sektorovich Grigorian, Valerik Telnovich Muradian, Armen Geverkovich Sayadian, Artash Tagikovich Epremian, Sarkis Cholokovich Akopian, Misak Surenovich Akanesian, Asatur Khristoforovich Khachaturian and Ashot Akopovich Tatevosian. As they could not be traced down, it was decided on June 19 1991 to suspend the investigation based on Article 209 section 1 of the Criminal Code.

The June 19 1991 decision to suspend the investigation on case no. 18/35208-91 was revoked by B. S. Mammadov, inspector of the Azeri Prosecutor General's special investigation team for priority cases, on the order of deputy Prosecutor General Khanlar Valiyev and the Military Prosecutor of the Republic of Azerbaijan on August 24 2005. The criminal case was updated and re-issued under criminal case no. 80377 of which the joint investigation team under the Military Prosecutor and the Prosecutor General of the Republic of Azerbaijan.

As part of the proceedings, the charges filed against the accused on December 18 and 20 1990 based on Article 220 section 1 of the Criminal Code were upheld.

The accused Manvel Sektorovich Grigorian, Valerik Telnovich Muradian, Armen Geverkovich Sayadian, Artash Tagikovich Epremian, Sarkis Cholokovich Akopian, Misak Surenovich Akanesian, Asatur Khristoforovich Khachaturian and Ashot Akopovich Tatevosian were hiding from justice, as a result of which it was impossible to put them under preventive detention. An arrest warrant for the group's members was issued on August 9 2005 by the Yasamal district court of Baku.

After the court's decision had come into force, a search order for the accused was issued on November 30 2005 by the First Deputy Military Prosecutor, who headed the joint investigation group with the Prosecutor General's office.

The investigation revealed that on the instruction of his superiors Mr. Grigorian, a member of the terrorist organization Ergraparkh (Ergrap), based on the territory of Armenia, had set up a terrorist cell composed of inhabitants of the Echmiadzin province of Armenia, which in November 1990 had been dispatched to Azerbaijan. The group had been instructed to carry out acts of terrorism and sabotage.

After its escape from justice, the Ergrap cell, also dubbed Echmiadzin military unit, had gathered strength and participated in killings of non-engaged Azeri citizens on the occupied territories. Its leader Manvel Grigorian was in the forefront of the armed campaigns against the Republic of Azerbaijan in the southern parts of Nagorno-Karabakh between 1988 and 1992. Grigorian and his unit were subordinate to the Ministry of Defence of Armenia, with Grigorian holding the rank of detachment commander. In 1992 he was appointed bridge commander, and in 1997 military unit commander. In 1996 by decree of the Republic of Armenia he was promoted to the rank of lieutenant-general while still remaining in command of Ergrap. In 2000 he was appointed deputy defence minister, a post which he held till 2008. At present he still heads the Ergrap unit and is the governor of the province of Echmiadzin. It is thus that a terrorist under charges in the Republic of Azerbaijan has been honoured with high ranks, positions and qualifications.

It is worth noting that in January 2001 a decree was signed by the President of Armenia, then Robert Kocharian, declaring May 8 the "Day of Ergrap and the liberation of Shusha" – pointing at the role the terrorist group has played in the occupation of Shusha. All this makes it undisputable that the Republic of Armenia is supporting terrorism.

Criminal case no. 80377/35277 in connection with armed attacks by Armenian groups and units in the district of Shusha

Criminal case no. 35277 was derived from an earlier case, no. 34625, filed on February 14 1991. Investigation material demonstrates that since 1988 non-engaged citizens in the city of Shusha in Nagorno-Karabakh have been the target of major-scale assaults, killings, injuries, hostage-taking and torture, with people homes burnt and their property looted, and families being chased from their native lands by Armenian armed paramilitary and military forces, forcing them to flee to Azerbaijan.

Criminal cases initiated by the Prosecutor's office of Shusha demonstrate that infantry units were involved in these crimes. Investigations resulted in a small number of Armenians being brought to justice and appearing in court. Criminal case no. 34625 developed into a co-ordinated investigation in a broader context against a number of individuals who were on the run from justice. The case concerned an attack carried out by Armenian terrorists who on January 9 1991 at 6.00hrs a.m. near kilometre mark 5 on the road between Lachin and Shusha took a military vehicle (number plate UAZ-469) belonging to military unit 44682 based in Ganja under fire, killing the driver sergeant Ivan Ivanivich Goek, reconnaissance battalion commander Oleg Mikhailovich Larionov, the military unit's chief of staff Igor Yuriyevich Ivanov and Mrs. Salatyn A. Askerova, journalist from the newspaper "Molodezh Azerbaijana".

Based on Article 209 section 1 (evasion from investigation and judicial proceedings or other grounds for failure to locate offenders) of the Criminal Code of the Republic of Azerbaijan, criminal proceedings concerning the case were suspended on February 14 1992.

On August 25 2005, however, the suspension of the case was revoked, the files were updated and the investigations resumed. The case was upgraded under Article 103 (genocide) of the Criminal Code. During the investigations, the file was sent to the Statistic Information Management Department of the Ministry of Internal Affairs of the Republic of Azerbaijan. In response, it would appear that in connection with the same criminal case 12 persons of Armenian nationality had been sentence to varying imprisonment terms by a court on March 23 1992.

On August 25 2005 arrest warrants were issued based on Article 103 of the Criminal Code for a number of persons evading the course of justice and previously identified as members of armed units. Their names were Zorik Shurikovich Gulian, Shirak Shogenovich Chobanian, Khachatur Sarkisovich Ohanesian, Valery Levonovich Balaian, Arut Gyorgievich Arutunian, Janna Gyorgievna Galustian, Deyran Surenovich Davidian, Vilen Arnodikovich Simonian, Slavik Bagratovich Grigorian, Grisha Aghabekovich Sarkisian, Andronik Pavlikovich Arutunian and Varujan Alexeyevich Nasibian. Required documentation was sent to the Yasamal district court in order to get warrants for their arrest, based on the court ruling made on August 26 2005 ordering their preventive detention. On November 21 2005, the court cleared the start of a search for them which was initiated by the authorities subsequently.

The attempt on the life of Major-General V. Kovaliyev, head of the internal affairs office of the Autonomous Region of Nagorno-Karabakh

On January 19 1991 the inhabitants of Khankendi V. Bagmanian, A. Antonian and S. Bagmanian carried out an attempt on the life of Major-General V. Kovaliyev, head of the internal affairs office of the Autonomous Region of Nagorno-Karabakh. Vladimir Vladimirovich Kovaliyev escaped unhurt. He was to be killed as one of the victims of the Armenian terrorists who shot down a helicopter MI-8 on November 20 1991 over the village of Garakend in the Nagorno-Karabakh region with a delegation of high-raking state officials on board all of whom were to perish.

Meanwhile, on April 8 1991, the head of the office of the internal forces of the USSR responsible for the Northern and the Southern Caucasus, Colonel V. Blakhotin, became the target of a terrorist attack in Rostov-on-Don, Russia. The Rostov court subsequently sentenced five criminals responsible for the attack to various terms in prison: 15 years each for V. Bagmanian and A. Antonian, 12 years for S. Bagmanian, 4 years for K. Akopian, and 2 years and 9 months for K. Yegitian.

Criminal case no. 80377/64510 in connection with an armed attack on a coach on the motorwar Agdam-Shusha

On March 14 1991, a passenger coach on the road from Agdam to Shusha with number plate PAZ-67273-58 was blown up by an armed group consisting of Yuri Osipovich Djangirian and accomplices, hidden under camouflage in a vineyard near a cemetery, as a result of which three persons were killed and two injured.

A criminal case was opened following the event by S. G. Amirian, prosecutor of Askeran, based on Article 94 (premeditated murder under aggravating conditions), in particular section 4 (killing of two persons or more) of the Criminal Code of the Republic of Azerbaijan. On March 15 1991, the case and its investigation were taken over by G. Safarov, inspector of the Prosecutor's office in Askeran.

On June 5 1991, V. Sirzanov, inspector of the investigation team of the department of internal affairs of the Autonomous Region of Nagorno-Karabakh, took charge of the criminal case.

As a result of a search campaign as part of investigations, on August 9 1991 Yuri Osipovich Djangirian, leader of the criminal group, was ararested and handed over to the investigation team, upon which V. Sirzanov ordered a continuation of the investigations. On August 12 1991, it was decided to keep Yuri Osipovich Djangirian in preventive detention and E. Ahmadov was put in charge of the investigations. The latter ordered, on October 9 1991, to include criminal case no. 33838, concerning the kidnapping and hostage-taking of Khanlar Shahmamadov by Yuri Djangirian, into the investigations and hadle the two files as a single case.

On December 31 1991, the criminal case concerning Yuri Osipovich Djangirian was taken to court, as a result of which the Supreme Court of the Republic of Azerbaijan sentenced him to death on April 2 1992.

On December 30 1991 based on material collected during investigations regarding case no. 33827/33838, investigations continued against other members of the group led by Yuri Djangirian. A new case was opened under no. 64510 based on Article 209 (evasion from investigation and judicial proceedings or other grounds for failure to locate offenders) and in particular section 1-3 (inability to identify perpetrators) of the Criminal Code of the Republic of Azerbaijan. On March 1 1992, the case was shelved.

On December 8 2003, however, by a joint decree of the Prosecutor General's office, the Ministry of Internal Affairs and the Ministry of National Security of the Republic of Azerbaijan, a joint investigation team was put on the criminal case once more as part of investigations into crimes committed by separatists of the Autonomous Region of Nagorno-Karabakh, and the decision made on March 1 1992 to shelve the case was revoked. Files were updated and the case was reopened under Articles 103 (genocide) and 107 (deportation) of the Criminal Code of the Republic of Azerbaijan.

Criminal case no. 24634/33020 in connection with the murder of employees of the Ministry of Internal Affairs

On February 18 1991 at 20.00hrs a coach of the type UAZ-452 with number plate 91-25 AQM driven by Alvan Arshad Aghayev and carrying Namig Hasan Hummatov, local police officer of the Internal Affairs Branch, militiaman Chingiz Arshad Ismayilov and soldier of military unit no. 3673 of the internal troops under the Ministry of Internal Affairs Aynur Rashidovich Imayev was taken under intensive gunfire in the district of Fizuli near the 300 kilometre mark at the Armenian church Amaras near the collective farm of Khodjavend. Hummatov, Imagyev and Aghayev were killed while Ismayilov and a fifth man named Shelnikov were injured.

Following the event, a criminal case was opened as of April 19 1991 by the prosecutor of Fizuli E. Majidov based on Article 94 section 2-4 (premeditated murder under aggravating conditions of two or more persons and seriously jeopardising human life) of the Criminal Code of the Republic of Azerbaijan.

On September 3 1991, proceedings were shelved based on Article 209 (inability to identify perpetrators) of the Criminal Code of the Republic of Azerbaijan.

Criminal case no. 35270 on the shoot-down of a helicopter MI-8 using firearms

On November 20 1991, a MI-8 helicopter carrying on board a group of distinguished state officials, politicians and high military officers of Azerbaijan, Kazakhstan, Russia accompanied by junior officials and journalists was shot down by Armenian terrorists over the settlement of Garakend in the region of Nagorno-Karabakh in Azerbaijan. As a result of the tragedy 22 persons perished:

Tofig Kazim Ismalyilov, State Secretary of the Republic of Azerbaijan

Ismat Ismail Gayibov, representative of the Azeri Prosecutor General's office

Zulfi Saleh Adjiyeva, depty Prime Minister of Azerbaijan

Nabi Mahammad Asadov, state adviser to the Republic of Azerbaijan

Vali Huseyn Mammadov, deputy of the USSR

Rafig Mammad Mammadov, assistant to the State Secretary of the Republic of Azerbaijan

Gurban Huseyn Namazaliyev, deputy Minister of Develop of the Republic of Azerbaijan

Osman Mirhuseyn, head of the Presidential Administration of the Republic of Azerbaijan

Vagif Djafar Djafarov, deputy Construction Minister of Azerbaijan

Fakhraddin Ibrahim Shahbazov, executive of the Broadcasting Company of the Republic of Azerbaijan

Arif Ismayil Huseynzadeh, , executive of the Broadcasting Company of the Republic of Azerbaijan

Ali Mustafa Mustafayev, , executive of the Broadcasting Company of the Republic of Azerbaijan

Igor Alexandrovich Plavsky, Prosecutor of the Autonomous Region of Nagorno-Karabakh

Vladimir Vladimirovich Kovaliyev, head of the Department of Internal Affairs of the Autonomous Region of Nagorno-Karabakh

Sergey Semyonovich Ivanov, chairman of the PSC of the Autonomous Region of Nagorno-Karabakh

Seilau Dosumovich Serikov, deputy Minister of Internal Affairs of the Republic of Kazakhstan

Mikhail Dmitryevich Lukashov, major-general, representative of the Socialist Republic of the Russian Federation

Nikolay Vladimirovich Jinkin, district special branch commander of the Autonomous Region of Nagorno-Karabakh

Oleg Nikolayevich Kocharov, colonel, Soviet army officer

Vyacheslav Vladimirovich Kotov, helicopter commander

Gennadi Vladimirovich Dolgov, helicopter crew member

Dmitriy Borisovich Yalovenko, Helicopter crew member

The mentioned victims' remains were taken from the site for forensic examination and evaluation of the event.

On November 21 1991 a criminal case was opened without specifying the article of the Criminal Code of the Republic of Azerbaijan it was based by I. A. Lazutkin, the prosecutor of the military garrison of Khankendi. On November 23, the case was handed over to the Prosecutor General's office for further investigation.

By a decree dated April 3 2002 the criminal act was classified under Article 59 (act of terrorism; in force until September 9 2000) of the Criminal Code of the Republic of Azerbaijan.

Initial investigations showed that the helicopter had been shot by three Armenian persons firing submachine and machine guns.

As a result, Benik Sandjanovich Abramian, living in Khodjavend, was arrested on suspicion of violating Article 70 (banditry; in force until September 9 2000) of the Criminal Code of the Republic of Azerbaijan by participating in illegal armed gangs' assaults on civilans.

During interrogations, Abramian alleged that the helicopter had been shot by three men, whose first names were Edik (who was also chairman of the Garakend village council), Robert (brought in for the purpose) and Lovik (a driver working in Khodjavend, using firearms.

For obvious reasons, it turned out to be impossible to identify these persons and take them in for interrogation.

Abramian was later exchanged for hostages in the hands of Armenian groups in the wake of the Khodjaly tragedy.

On December 31 1994 the preliminary investigation into the case was shelved in accordance with Article 209 (inability to identify perpetrators; in force until September 9 2000) of the Criminal Code of the Republic of Azerbaijan on the decision of N. I. Abbasov, inspector for serious crime investigations at the Prosecutor General's office.

Criminal case no. 64516 on yet another helicopter shoot-down

On January 28 1992 around 16.00hrs, a civilian helicopter was shot down while flying over the Agdam-Shusha motorway by Armenian terrorists, killing all three crew members and 39 passengers on board. The same day, a criminal case on the event was opened by F. I. Huseynov, , senior inspector of the department for high-priority investigations at the Prosecutor General's office, based on Article 70 (banditry) and Article 94 section 2-4 (premeditated murder under aggravating conditions of two or more persons and seriously jeopardising human life) of the Criminal Code of the Republic of Azerbaijan.

In the course of investigations it appeared that the civilian helicopter which belonged to the transportation service Azalpanx resorting under the Zabrat air company, a subsidiary of Azerbaijan's national flag-carrier Azal, was shot down by Armenian terrorists using firearms in the area of Khankendi, after which it crashed and exploded near the village of Gaybali, in the district of Shusha. All on board perished: captain Viktor Vasilyevich Seregin, pilot Safa Fatulla Akhundov, and board mechanic Arastun Isfandiyar Mahmudov, as well as 39 passengers the following were later identified: Shahin Ali Abbasov, Sadagat Kamran Abbasova, Saadat Shahin Abbasova, Hafiza Vali Gasimova, Khuraman Eldar Allahverdiyeva, Ekrem Khosrov Zalov, Bahar Isa Zalova, Namig Ekrem Zalov, Eldar Musa Guliyev, Murshud Amrali Dunyamaliyev, Sara Asif Aliyeva, Fazil Khazri Azizov, Zaur Kamal Guliyev, Sarkhan Dayandur Ismayilov, Shahin Huseyn Lazgiyev, Saleh Shahlar Huseynov, Parviz Shamsaddin Abbasov, Ridvan Yusif Veliyev, Asif Garakishi Garayev, Raifa Asif Garayeva, Saleh Asif Garayev, Asif Garaja Garayev, Telman Gahraman Ismayilov, Fikret Burza Mehdiyev, Bahram Metleb Ismayilov, Shakir Shaumyan Salahov, Vagif Alish Javadov,Djabbarov Khidir Sadraddin Djabbarov, Ramila Ibrahim Zeynalova Djamal Ali , Hasanov, Sevindiyev Arshad Gara Sevindiyev, Roza Rehber Djabbarova, Niyazi Veliyaddin Mammadov, and Zakir Mehman Mammadov.

On April 28 1991 the case was shelved in accordance with Article 209 (inability to identify perpetrators) of the Criminal Code of the Republic of Azerbaijan.

Terrorist acts committed by Armenian activists related to the Nagorno-Karabakh conflict outside the fighting zone

Criminal case no. 140 in connection with the explosion of a coach on route 106 in Baku

On September 8 1984, a criminal case was opened based on Article 15 section 91 (deliberate attempt to inflict damage on state and public property) and Article 94 section 6 (premeditated murder under aggravating conditions of two or more persons and seriously jeopardising human life; in vigour till September 1 2000) of the Criminal Code of the Republic of Azerbaijan by A. T. Zamanov, then Prosecutor General of the Republic of Azerbaijan, following the explosion of a coach on route 106. Investigations into the event were in the hands of the all Union KGB.

In the course of the investigations it was discovered that the act of terrorism had been carried out by an Armenian called Henrikh Surenovich Vartanov with the help of a Russian called Igor Mikhailovic Makhovsky born in 1960. Both were inhabitants of Baku.

In his testimony Makhovsky was to declare that he had met Vartanov incidentally at a bus stop in Baku. At their next meeting, Vartanov had requested him to prepare an explosion device with a time clock which Makhovsky accepted. Earlier in 1984, Makhovsky had made a few test explosions in the basement of Vartanov's home. On September 8 1984 at noon, Vartanov took the explosive device which Makhovsky had given him to the last bus stop at Route 106 in the district of Montino and placed it between seats 5 and 6 of a coach of the type Ikarus-28001 with number plate 90-11 AQ. At 13.50, the bus exploded in front of the Polytechnic Institute.

As a result of the explosion, a woman by the name of F. I. Surkhalizadeh was killed and three persons, G. D. Mansurova, T. Kh. Mehtiyeva and E. S. Zorin, were injured.

On March 15 1985 Igor Mikhailovich Makhovsky was sentenced to 15 imprisonment by the Supreme Court of the Republic of Azerbaijan based on Articles 15, 17 and 94 section 6 (premeditated murder under aggravating conditions of two or more persons and seriously jeopardising human life; in vigour till September 1 2000) of the Criminal Code of the Republic of Azerbaijan.

As for Vartanov, who was the perpetrator of the terrorist act, the Supreme Court of the USSR released him from custody on March 15 1985, following a diagnosis of schizophrenia which declared him not responsible for his criminal acts, based on Articles 396 and 397 of the Criminal Code. It is obvious that Armenians holding high positions in the USSR had the power to influence such decisions.

This serious crime has been the first act of terror carried out on the territory of Azerbaijan towards the end of the XX Century.

Criminal case no. 11 in connection with the explosion of a coach on the track Baku-Tbilisi

On September 16 1989 around 13.00hrs a coach of the type Ikarus-256 with number plate 80-09 AQP and driven by citizen Firuz Maharram Bayramov was blasted by unknown persons on the motorway between Tbilisi and Baku at the 285 kilometre mark, causing serious loss of life, killing 5 and injuring 26 of the 53 passengers on board.

Following the event, the same day a criminal case was opened by the district prosecutor of Yevlakh based on Article 61 (sabotage; in force until Sepbemter 1 2000) of the Criminal Code of the Republic of Azerbaijan.

On May 7 1990, the case was shelved in accordance with Article 209 (inability to identify perpetrators) of the Criminal Code of the Republic of Azerbaijan by S. Bayramov, senior inspector for priority cases of the criminal investigation department of the KGB.

Criminal case no. 32053 connected with an armed attack on the settlement of Sederek, Sharur district, Nakhchivan

On January 19 1990, the settlement of Sederek located in the district of Sharur in the Autonomous Republic of Nakhchivan on Azeri territory, came under attack by Armenian extremists coming from the districts Ararat (Devely) and Yerashk (Arazdeyen) on the territory of the Republic of Armenia. The same day, a criminal case was opened by V. Ahmadov, senior inspector under the Prosecutor's office in the district of Sharur, based on Article 94 sections 4 and 6 (premeditated murder under aggravating conditions of two or more persons and seriously jeopardising human life; in vigour till September 1 2000) as well as Article 91 (repeated deliberate attempts with serious consequences to inflict destruction and damage upon state and public property) of the Criminal Code of the Republic of Azerbaijan.

Investigations were to produce evidence contributed by witnesses that on January 19 1990 the settlement of Sederek located in the district of Sharur in the Autonomous Republic of Nakhchivan was taken under attack by Armenian extremists coming from the districts Ararat (Devely) and Yerashk (Arazdeyen) on the territory of the Republic of Armenia. It started by firing various types of guns and artillery, followed by the seizure and destruction of a nearby wine factory. As a result of the attack and of the artillery shelling, 7 persons were

33

killed: Maharram Miraziz Seyidov, chief constable of the Sharur district police, Mirsamil Mirshahin Seyidov, Etibar Rsagulu Ahmadov, Mammad Ail Mammadov, Ilgar Alasgar Mammadov, and two brothers aged 5 and 8 Elvin and Malik Tofig Nasirov who were playing in a courtyard and hit by artillery shell fragments. 25 more people suffered from injuries of varying seriousness. Armenian extremists also shelled district school no. 1 at Sederek. The pupils were swiftly evacuated and no one got hurt, but the school caught fire and was seriously damaged.

On June 4 1990, the case was shelved in accordance with Article 209 (inability to identify perpetrators) of the Criminal Code of the Republic of Azerbaijan.

Criminal case connected with the murder of colonel V. Blakhotin, deputy chief commander of the internal forces in the Northern and Southern Caucasus of the Ministry of Internal Affairs of the USSR

Armenians must have decided the physical destruction of V. Safonov, military commander of the Autonomous Region of Nagorno-Karabakh since he was in charge of disarmament of Armenian groups in the region. But on April 8 1991 in Rostov-on-Don, Russia, in what was intended as an attempt on his life instead they accidentally murdered colonel V. Blakhotin, deputy chief commander of the internal forces in the Northern and Southern Caucasus of the Ministry of Internal Affairs of the USSR.

In connection with the event a criminal case was opened by the regional court of Rostov. As a result, the following terrorists were sentenced to various prison terms: 15 years for A. Bagmanian, 12 years for S. Bagmanian, 4 years for K. Akopian, and 2 years and 9 months for K. Yegitian.

Criminal case connected with the assassination of Russian military officer V. P. Polyanichko, head of the Reorganisation Committee for Nagorno-Karabakh

On May 9 1991, a first attack on the Russian military officer was carried out in Khankendi. The attempt failed, but on August 1 1993 Viktor Petrovich Polyanichko, head of the Reorganisation Committee for Nagorno-Karabakh, was killed in the Russian federal republic of North-Ossetia (Alania).

The victim had gone out for a conversation with Ossetian field commanders when his service car was taken under gunfire by unknown people. Forensic inspection showed 15 bullet wounds in Polyanichko's body. Also killed in the act were major-general Anatoli Korechsky, commander of the 42nd Army Corps and chief commander of the Russian federal troops at the garrison of Vladikavkaz, as well as senior lieutenant Viktor Kravchuk, in command of the anti-terror unit Alpha. Four other people were injured. Neither were the culprits identified, nor was the motive for the murder officially established.

Bitish journalist Thomas de Waal in his book Black Garden: through peace and war alleges that "Polyanichko was killed as a result of an attack by Armenian terrorists in the North Caucasus". Andrey Girenko, former Secretary on Nationality Issues of the Central Committee of the Communist Party of the Soviet Union was to declare in an interview to the newsreel Vesti.az that Polyanichko's position had always been that whatever happened, Nagorno-Karabakh should be preserved as part of the Republic of Azerbaijan – hence the assassination attempt by Armenians in Khankendi while he was on duty.

V. V. Krivopuskov, a member of the investigation unit within the Ministry of Internal Affairs of the USSR, wrote in December

1990 that there had been three attempts on Polyanichko's life in Karabakh by Armenians. In the first attempt, a truck pushed his car into a ravine, but he was not inside. The next time, a bomb exploded in a train after it entered the railway station. But as Polyanichko had left the train before the blast, he escaped unharmed. The third time, he had an even narrower escape, as while attending a meeting in his office room with the Executive Committee of the Autonomous Region of Nagorno-Karabakh a grenade was fired with a launcher from the park opposite the building through the window. Viktor Petrovich had a heavy contusion and hurt his ears, but his life was saved. 27)

Criminal charges were filed and an investigation initiated following the murder of Polyanichko in North Ossetia by the law enforcement agencies of the Russian Federation.

The explosion on the train Moscow-Baku

On May 30 1991 an explosion occurred on the passenger train from Moscow to Baku near the railway station of Khasavyurd in the Russian federal republic of Dagestan, causing the deaths of 11 people and leaving 22 injured. A criminal case was filed and investigations were carried out by the law enforcement agencies of the Russian Federation. 28)

A second explosion on the train Moscow-Baku

On July 31 1991 a second explosion occurred on the passenger train from Moscow to Baku near the railway station of Khasavyurd in the Russian federal republic of Dagestan, causing the deaths of 11 people and leaving 22 injured. A criminal case was filed and investigations were carried out by the law enforcement agencies of the Russian Federation. 29)

Criminal case no. 39967 in relation to a terrorist act on the ferryboat Sovietskaya Kalmykaya

On January 8 1992 a bomb exploded on a ferryboat sailing from Krasnovodsk to Baku, killing 23 and injuring 80. On September 1, criminal charges were brought by Ch. M. Seyfullayev, prosecutor of the South Caspian offshore water transportation area. Investigations pointed at Armenians having arrived in Baku by boat more than once. Expertise confirmed that the explosion was the result of an act of terrorism. But the culprits could not be found, and as a result the case was shelved in accordance with Article 209 (inability to identify perpetrators) of the Criminal Code of the Republic of Azerbaijan.

The explosion on the passenger train Kislovodsk-Baku

On February 28 1993, an explosion occurred on the passenger train from Kislovodsk to Baku near the railway station of Gudermes in the northern Caucasus, Russia. As a result of the explosion 13 persons died and 12 were injured. A criminal case was filed and investigations were carried out by the law enforcement agencies of the Russian Federation. 30)

Criminal case no. 201 in relation to the explosion on the train from Baku to Astara

On February 1 1994 around 22.45hrs an act of terror took place in the form of a bomb explosion on train no. 66 with carriages 055, 24533 and 25193 from Baku to Astara, leaving 3 dead – Shabeyim Alaga Djamalova, Afet Maksud Mirzayev and Shafiga Mammadali Aliyeva – while injuring a number of others and causing major damage to state property.

The following day, a criminal case was opened based on Article 61 (sabotage) of the Criminal Code of the Republic of Azerbaijan by R. Mansurov, chief inspector at the investigation department of the Ministry of National Security of the Republic of Azerbaijan.

On December 31 1994 the case was shelved in accordance with Article 209 (inability to identify perpetrators) of the Criminal Code of the Republic of Azerbaijan.

Criminal case no. 90013 related to the explosion of a freight train at the station of Khudat

On February 9 1994 at 20.40hrs a freight train, parked off the main track near the station of Khudat at the border between Dagestan and Azerbaijan was blown up. Fortunately, the train was empty and nobody was hurt. A criminal case was opened based on Article 61 (sabotage; in vigour till September 1 2000) of the Criminal Code of the Republic of Azerbaijan by A. G. Hamidov, prosecutor for transportation of Kachmaz. In the course of investigations it would appear that the explosion occurred through an explosive device which had been placed on the train in advance. As the culprits could not be traced, the case was shelved in accordance with Article 209 (inability to identify perpetrators) of the Criminal Code of the Republic of Azerbaijan.

The shoot-down of a Hercules aircraft

On March 17 1994, an airplane, type Hercules C-130 belonging to the Iranian military air force was shot down near the town of Khankendi, killing 32 diplomats on board and their 19 family members including 9 children.

According to Armenian officials, the aircraft was supposed to follow its course over the territories of Russia, Georgia and Armenia. But it deviated from its course around 100 kilometre towards the south and instead of for Armenia it headed for the combat zone of the Autonomous Region of Nagorno-Karabakh, circumventing Armenian territory.

Armenia's vice-President Gagik Arutyunian claimed that the airplane crashed because of a malfunctioning navigating system but the Iranian side refuted that explanation. Representatives of the Iranian Foreign Ministry declared that the "airplane exploded after having deviated from its course". A commission created by the Iranians to investigate into the matter concluded that the plane had been shot down by two missiles fired from Armenian military positions who had taken it for an Azeri aircraft – hence the fact that they had sent no warning signals to the crew. The Armenian side refused to assume any responsibility for the incident, even though at a later stage Armenia's vice President Gagik Arutyunian admitted that the Iranian airplane had been "shot down by mistake". 31)

Criminal case no. 212234 related to the bomb explosion at the Baku underground station 20 January

On March 19 1994 14 people perished and 56 others were injured in an explosion ripping through the Baku underground station 20 January. Following investigations, a suspect by the name of Rahib Shaval Maksimov, an ethnic Lezghian, was arrested on July 29 1994 and charged with the act of terrorism.

Following the incident, 60 persons were interrogated, 44 forensic examinations were carried out as a result of which the perpetrator of the terrorist act Alfet Khalid Sefereliyev was identified upon which he was arrested on November 10 in accordance with Article 220 (illegal possession of firearms and explosives and there purchase and preparation for action) of the Criminal Code of the Republic of Azerbaijan.

As a result of investigations evidence was collected proving that R. Sh. Maksimov together with other accomplices had been working as a team in planning to commit acts of mass destruction in Baku with the aim to undermine the state of Azerbaijan during the month of February 1994.

On December 8 1994, Ruslan Danyal Rahimkhanov, born 1960, was arrested in the village of Avaran in the district of Gusar and put under accusation.

As a result of investigations it was established that together with Telman Sirajaddin Suleymanov, Rahib Shaval Maksimov had set up a criminal group further consisting of A. Kh. Sefereliyev, R. D. Rahimkhanov and others with the aim to commit acts of terrorism. By the end of February 1994, Rahib Shaval Maksimov, Telman Sirajaddin Suleymanov and others had gathered in the restauranat Shahnabat in the Gusar district where they discussed the details of the intended terrorist crime in Baku.

On March 19 1994 Maksimov, Suleymanov, Sefereliyev and two men identified as E. Sh. Orudjov and Asef put four packages of explosives in the back of a Djiguly car and drove it to Baku. At 13.00hrs they met with Oktay Gurbanov, in inhabitant of the town of Gusar, near the 20 January underground station. O. Gurbanov took one package containing explosives and went into the underground station while Maksimov prepared another package which he had kept. At 13.55hrs 800 gramme TNT of explosives went off, causing grave loss of human life. The other members of the group Sefereliyev and Orudjov refused to proceed and cause further explosions at the Nizami underground station and the Republic Palace in Baku and thereby thwarted further acts of terror.

It was to be proven in court that though the act of terror was carried out by the Lezghian separatist organisation Sadval, its preparation had been in close cooperation with Armenian special services. It was demonstrated that activists of Sadval had repeatedly visited Armenia since 1992 and received money, organisational support and arms supplies from the Armenian General National Security Unit. In late April and May 1992, ethnic Lezghians of Azeri nationality received special training in terrorism and sabotage on a base located in the settlement of Lusakert in the Nairi province in Armenia. Investigations were to reveal that according to their instructions, apart from the January 20 underground station, the saboteurs intended to set off explosions at the Nizami cinema, the Republic Palace and the Baku bulb factory.

The conclusions resulted in a criminal case based on Articles 61 (sabotage) and 94 (premeditated murder under aggravating conditions) of the Criminal Code of the Republic of Azerbaijan, assigned to the Baku city prosecutor's office. The file was also sent for further investigation to the Ministry of National Security of the Republic of Azerbaijan. On May 3, the Supreme Court of the Republic of Azerbaijan convicted Rahib Shaval Maksimov and Telman Sirajaddin Suleymanov to 15 years in prison each, while other members including R. N. Baghiyev and M. S. Zohrabov were sentenced to 14 years in prison each.

One more explosion on the passenger train Moscow-Baku

On April 13 1994 an explosion occurred on the passenger train from Moscow to Baku near the railway station Dagestanskaya Ogni in the Republic of Dagestan, as a result of which three people died and another three were injured. A criminal case was opened and investigations started by the law enforcement agencies of the Russian Federation. 32)

Criminal case no. 208 related to an explosion at the Baku railway station

On April 27 1994, a criminal case was opened against Igor Anatoliyevich Khatkovsky based on Articles 58 (espionage), 61 (sabotage) and 220 section 2 (illegal possession of firearms and explosives and there purchase and preparation for action) of the Criminal Code of the Republic of Azerbaijan, derived from an earlier case filed under no. 190 against Djagan Anushavanovich Ohanesian, Boris Vazgenovich Simonian and Ashot Aratovich Goloian based on Articles 17.51 (collaboration with espionage) 17.15.61 (preparation of and participation in sabotage) as well as Articles 17 and 67 section 3 (racial discrimination and killing under aggravating conditions respectively) of the Criminal Code of the Republic of Azerbaijan.

Preliminary investigations were to show that in February 1993 I. Khatkovsky came to Yerevan where he met the head of the Armenian railway security service. He was subsequently recruited by the head of the Directorate of National Security (former KGB) of Armenia, lieutenant-colonel Djagan Anushavanovich Ohanesian, who was personally involved in a unit known under its code name Kotovsky and created to organise subversive and terrorist operations on the territory of Azerbaijan. Khatkovsky worked closely together with major Ashot Aratovich Goloian, agent of the Armenian Directorate of National Security, and with Boris Vazgenovich Simonian. They gave detailed instructions to Khatkovsky on how to organise bombings of transportation and communication facilities and other vital services in Azerbaijan.

In the instructions of Djagan Anushavanovich Ohanesian, Boris Vazgenovich Simonian and Ashot Aratovich Goloian, Khatkovsky gathered information on the social, political and economic situation in Azerbaijan, as well as the government and political leaders of the country, schedules for trains moving from the Russian Federation into Azerbaijan, border, passport and customs control procedures, locations of important transportation hubs and engineering installations, oil and gas pipelines and electric power lines along railway tracks, and further information about particular individuals living in Baku. By the end of May 1993, Djagan Anushavanovich Ohanesian and Ashot Aratovich Goloian met with Khatkovsky at the Ani hotel in Yerevan and gave him explosive devices and other equipment needed to commit terrorist attacks on the territory of Azerbaijan, at least part of which he took with him to Baku.

While shuttling between Yerevan and Baku, Khatkovsky passed on the information he gathered on to Ohanesian, for whom he prepared several detailed reports in writing. In compensation and repayment for his expenses during stays in Moscow and Yerevan during the months of February and March 1993, Khatkovsky received payments from Djagan Anushavanovich Ohanesian, Boris Vazgenovich Simonian and Ashot Aratovich Goloian to a total amount of 470,000 Russian rouble.

As a result of it all, passenger rail car no. 13841 standing alongside platform 5 at the central railway station of Baku was blown up using 9 pieces of 200 gramme explosives, 2 other packages of explosives and 2 landmines on that fateful day in May 1993 at 21.30hrs.

On June 22 1994 charges were filed against Djagan Anushavanovich Ohanesian, Boris Vazgenovich Simonian and Ashot Aratovich Goloian, based on Articles 17.51 (collaboration with espionage) 17.15.61 (preparation of and participation in sabotage) as well as Articles 17 and 67 section 3 (racial discrimination and killing under aggravating conditions respectively) of the Criminal Code of the Republic of Azerbaijan.

It would take until April 5, though, before the culprits were put in custody and under accusation, followed by charges filed on September 4 1996

Following the attack, files connected with it were sent by the Prosecutor General's office of Azerbaijan to his peer in the Russian Federation on October 5 1993 and February 16 1994.

On May 12 1994, Djagan Anushavanovich Ohanesian, Boris Vazgenovich Simonian and Ashot Aratovich Goloian were arrested in Moscow and on the following May 20 a criminal case was opened against the three by the Chief Military Prosecutor of the Russian Federation.

On March 11 1996, the court of the military garrison of Tambov found K. Katkovsky guilty of the explosion that had occurred on May 19 1993 when a freight train at the station of Derbent (Dagestan, Russia) had been blown up, illegal possession and purchase of firearms, ammunition and explosives, all with assistance of the Directorate for National Security (former KGB) of Armenia, referring to Articles 15 section 86 (destruction of roads and means of transportation) and 218 (illegal possession of ammunition) of the Penal Code of the Russian Federation. Djagan Anushavanovich Ohanesian was convicted to 6 years, Boris Vazgenovich Simonian to 2 years and Ashot Aratovich Goloian to 1 year and 6 months in prison.

A request to bring Ohanesian and Goloian to justice in Azerbaijan was turned down by the Russian Federation.

On September 5 1996 the case was shelved in accordance with Article 209 (inability to identify perpetrators) of the Criminal Code of the Republic of Azerbaijan.

On October 19 2006, however, the decision of September 5 1996 was revoked by the Prosecutor General and the Military Prosecutor of the Republic of Azerbaijan. Files were updated and proceedings resumed, as a result of which on April 18 2003 further investigations were assigned to I. Mammadov, the head of the joint investigation team on crimes committed by armed separatist forces of Nagorno-Karabakh and Armenian armed forces.

The same day, charges were filed based on Article 214 section 1 (terrorism) of the Criminal Code of the Republic of Azerbaijan and preventive arrest warrants were issued by the Yasamal district court of the City of Baku.

Criminal case no. 68477 related to the explosion on the Baku underground between the stations 28 May and Gandjlik

On July 3 1994 at 8.30hrs 13 persons were killed and 42 injured to varying degrees as a result of an explosion on the Baku underground between the stations 28 May and Gandjlik.

The same day, a criminal case was opened by the Prosecutor General's office based on Articles 61 (sabotage) and 220 section 2 (illegal possession of firearms and explosives and there purchase and preparation for action) of the Criminal Code of the Republic of Azerbaijan.

In connection with the crime, Azer Salman Aslanov was arrested on October 3 1994 by the law enforcement agencies of the Russian Federation under Article 213 section 3 paragraph 3 of the Criminal Code of the Russian Federation. On November 29 1997, the file on criminal case no. 97 was sent by the Federal Security Service to the office of the Prosecutor General of the Republic of Azerbaijan with the intention to combine the case with investigations carried out in Azerbaijan.

Investigations were to demonstrate that the act of terror had been committed by Azar Salman-oglu Aslanov, citizen of the Republic of Azerbaijan, who had been taken prisoner on January 13 1994 during a military clash at Daghlig Garabagh after which he got engaged in secret cooperation with Armenian special services. In captivity, Azar Aslanov, now prisoner of war and of Lezghian ethnic origin, met with writer Zori

Balaian, one of the Armenian separatists' ideologists, who talked into him about the importance of national minorities' cooperation in joint activities against Azeris. On June 9 1994, an Armenian agent calling himself Arthur telephoned to A. Aslanov's flat in Baku, telling his family that Azar was alive and urging that one of his relative should travel to Yerevan in order to arrange his release.

It was thus that Tadjibat Aslanova, Azar Aslanov's mother, arrived in Yerevan on June 16 1994. Azar Aslanov was told that his mother's life was under threat since he was involved in permanent cooperation with an Armenian special service unit operating under the code name Omar-75. Forged documents were prepared on his name. Explosives were hidden in chocolate boxes and deodorant bottles under his coat as he set off to penetrate into Azerbaijan. Aslanov arrived in Azerbaijan along the road Yerevan-Mineralnye Vodiy-Baku, ending in the terrorist attack on the Baku underground between the stations 28 May and Gandjlik, after which he returned to Yerevan. His mother, who had been held as a hostage during that time, was released.

During investigations it became apparent that the act of terror had been carried out under instructions of colonel Karen Bagdasarian and captain Seyran Sarkisian, both employees of the Armenian special services. Investigations proved Azara Aslanov guilty upon which charges were filed based on Articles 57 (treason), 61 (sabotage), 71 (smuggling), 17 section 94 paragraph 4 (premeditated murder under aggravating conditions) of the Criminal Code of the Republic of Azerbaijan at the Supreme Court of the Republic of Azerbaijan, which sentence him to life in prison. On April 26 1998 the case was shelved in accordance with Article 209 (inability to identify perpetrators) of the Criminal Code of the Republic of Azerbaijan by the Supreme Court.

During judicial proceedings carried out by the Supreme Court of the Republic of Azerbaijan it was established that Zori Balaian had been the initiator of the act of terror and a criminal case was opened based on Articles 17 section 61 (participation in sabotage) and section 94 paragraph 4 (premeditated murder under aggravating conditions) of the Criminal Code of the Republic of Azerbaijan. On April 9 1988 the results of the investigation were submitted to the to the office of the Prosecutor General of the Republic of Azerbaijan.

On May 9 1998, files were combined into an integrated case and on June 9 1998 charges were filed based on Articles 57 (treason), 61 (sabotage), 71 (smuggling), 17 section 94 paragraph 4 (premeditated murder under aggravating conditions) of the Criminal Code of the Republic of Azerbaijan against Zori Gaykovich Balaian and Karen Robikovich Bagdasarian. Warrants for their preventive arrest were issued.

Since it was impossible to locate Balaian and other suspects, the case was shelved in accordance with Article 209 (inability to identify perpetrators) of the Criminal Code of the Republic of Azerbaijan.

On May 11 2004, however, the investigation team received a letter from the Ministry of National Security of the Republic of Azerbaijan. In the letter, dated May 5 2004, it was noted that on July 3 1994 a person known as Levon had been acting as one of the agents doing research on how to carry out the terrorist attack on the Baku underground, had been identified as Levon Vagarshakovich Mirzoian, born in 1965 or 1967 in the village Dashalty, in the district of Shusha, now under Armenian occupation. Though still an Azeri citizen, he had been living in the town of Khankendi, 29 Uzbekistan Street.

Based on this information, the dismissal of case no. 68447 that had been decided on December 30 2003 was revoked. On June 15 2004 the deputy Chief Prosecutor of the Republic of Azerbaijan appointed M. Djabbarov, the head of the joint investigation team, to proceed with investigations.

Following investigations were to reveal that the Azeri citizen Levon Vagarshakovich Mirzoian had intentionally sided with the enemy with the aim to undermine the defence capacity and economic security of the Republic of Azerbaijan, assisted by Zori Gaykovich Balaian, Karen Robikovich Bagdasarian and other members of special branch offices of the Republic of Armenia and Nagorno-Karabakh, to prepare and carry out bombings of transportation and communication facilities, carry out premeditated murders of more than one persons and hit crucial services in Azerbaijan.

Investigations established that Mirzoian lived in the town of Khankendi on the territory of Azerbaijan but occupied by Armenian forces due to which it was impossible to bring him to justice to respond for his crimes.

Nevertheless, on June 11 2004 charges were filed based on Articles 32 section 120.2.7 (involvement in premeditated murder of two or more persons), 274 (high treason) and 32 section 282 (involvement in sabotage), of the Criminal Code of the Republic of Azerbaijan against Levon Mirzoian. On June 17 2004, the Sabail district court of the City of Baku issues an arrest warrant against him.

Criminal case no. 69537 in relation to the bombing scheme at the Taza Pir mosque

On June 30 1994, Roman Anatoliyevich Orekhov, born 1968, was detained by police near the mosque Taza Pir in the city of Baku as a suspect in connection with investigations into criminal case no. 68447 related to the explosion on the Baku underground between the stations 28 May and Gandjlik back in 1994, and was brought in for interrogation.

In the course of the interrogation Roman Orekhov admitted that he had been involved in terrorist acts in cooperation with and on the instructions of Armenians. In connection with this, criminal case no. 69537 had been opened by N. M. Hasanov, head of the investigation team under the Prosecutor General of the Republic of Azerbaijan, on December 29 1994.

While interrogated, Orekhov informed that he had met with two men who presented themselves as Armenians under the surnames Romik and Garik in the city of Rostov. Knowing that he was unemployed, they first offered him 5,000 US dollar to come and "fight in Nagorno-Karabakh". Later on, they revealed their real purpose, which was to send him down to commit terrorist acts. He accepted the offer and on June 17 1994 he arrived at Siyazan by train. He was supposed to meet with an old comrade together with whom he had served in the Soviet army by the name of Sh. Aliyev. He stayed a few days with him in Siyazan, after which he went on to Baku with the instruction to poison the water reservoir and have a bomb exploded during prayers at the Taza Pir mosque.

The Supreme Court of the Republic of Azerbaijan sentenced Roman Anatoliyevich Orekhov to 8 years in prison.

Photo 1. *September 16,1989 committed terrorism act passenger bus "Tbilisi-Baku"*

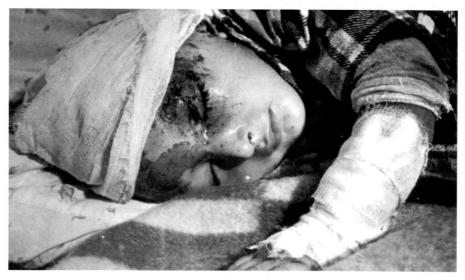

Photo 2. *Victim of September 16, 1989 committed terrorism act passenger bus "Tbilisi-Baku".*

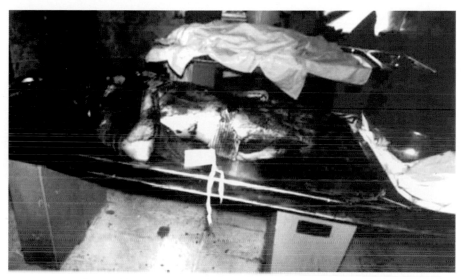

Photo 3. Victim of September 16, 1989 committed terrorism act passenger bus "Tbilisi-Baku"

Photo 4. February 18, 1990 committed terrorism act passenger bus "Shusha-Baku"

Photo 5. August 10, 1990 committed terrorism act passenger bus "Tbilisi-Aghdam".

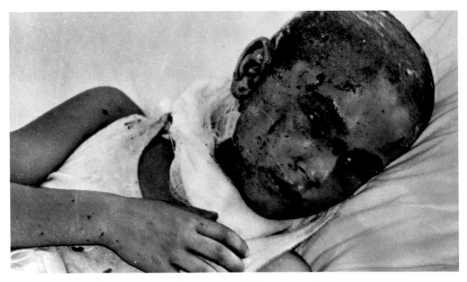

*Photo 6. Victim of August 10, 1990 committed terrorism act
passenger bus "Tbilisi-Aghdam".*

*Photo 7. Victim of August 10, 1990 committed terrorism act
passenger bus "Tbilisi-Aghdam"*

*Photo 8. January 9, 1991 committed terrorism act against a journalist from the newspaper
"Molodezh Azerbaijana" Mrs. S.A.Askerova and three Russian militaries.*

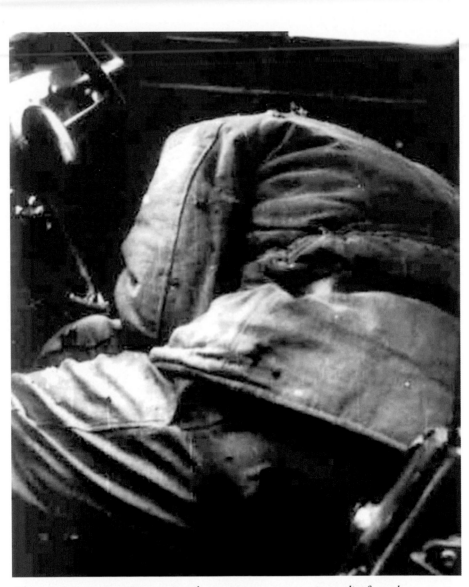

*Photo 9. January 9, 1991 committed terrorism act against a journalist from the newspaper
"Molodezh Azerbaijana" Mrs.S.A.Askerova and three Russian militaries*

Photo 10. May 30, 1991 committed terrorism act on a passenger train from Moscow to Baku near Khasavyurt station (Dagestan, Russian Federation).

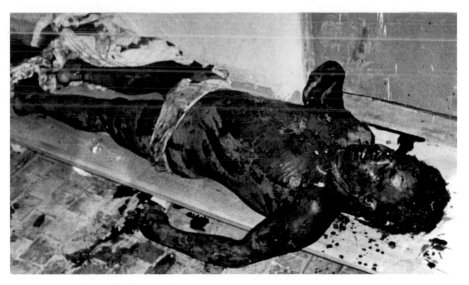

Photo 11. Victim of committed terrorist acts on a passenger train"
Moscow-Baku" near Temirtau station of Dagestan, Russian Federation

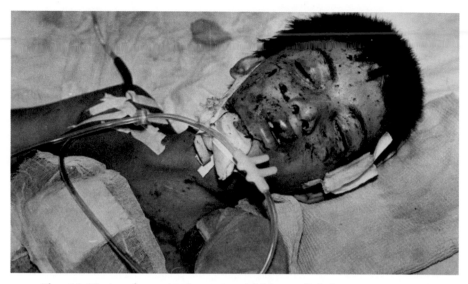

Photo12. Victim of committed terrorist acts" Moscow-Baku" passenger train was blown up near Temirtau station of Dagestan, Russian Federation

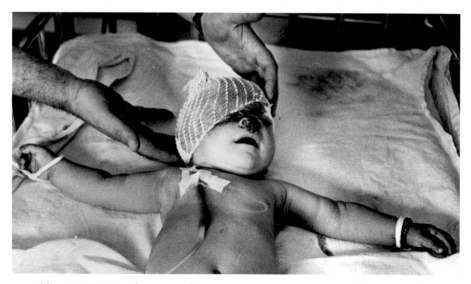

Photo 13. Victim of committed terrorist acts on a passenger train" Moscow-Baku" near Temirtau station of Dagestan, Russian Federation

Photo 14. November 20, 1991 "MI-8" helicopter was shot down near
village of Garakend in Khodjavend by Armenian terrorists

Photo 15. November 20, 1991 "MI-8" helicopter was shot down near
village of Garakend in Khodjavend by Armenian terrorists

Photo 16. January 8, 1992 committed terrorist act on "Krasnavodsk-Baku" ship.

Photo 17. January 8, 1992 committed terrorist act on "Krasnavodsk-Baku" ship.

Photo 18. February 1, 1994 committed terrorist act on a train "Kislovodsk - Baku"
train Baku railway station

Photo 19. March 19, 1990. Committed terrorist act "20 January"
in Baku underground station

Photo 20. 19 March 19, 1990. Committed terrorist act "20 January" in Baku underground station

Photo 21. 3 July, 1994.comitted terrorist act on a train between the 28 May and "Gyandjlik" underground stations.

*Photo 22. 3 July, 1994 comitted terrorist act on a train between the 28 May
and "Gyandjlık" underground stations.*

Confirmative photo facts committed genocide
against civilian population in Khojaly city.

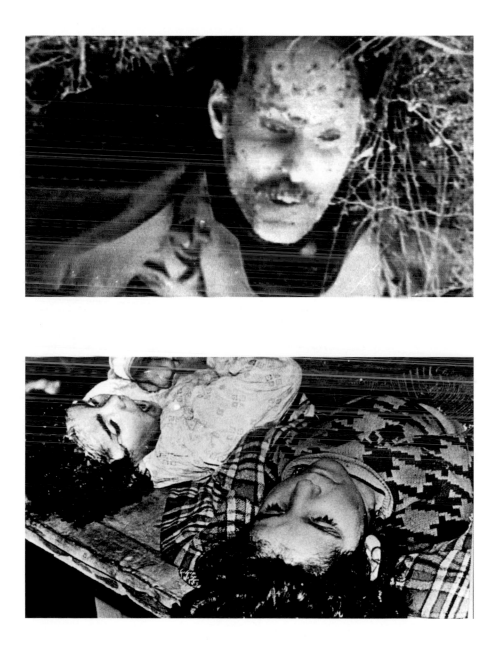

Photo: Viktoria Ivleva. *This morning was such in Khojaly. In Khojaly city, near their houses Armenian are looting their properties and carrying over the not cooled dead bodies of killed Azerbaijanis. This is "an ancient and civilized nation" of the word.*

Bibliography

Sources:

1. Relevant materials (about 1993 - 2014) of the State Commission on prisoners of war, hostages and missing persons;
2. Relevant achieve materials of the Ministry of National Security;
3. Criminal case No. 11;
4. Criminal case No. 38;
5. Criminal case No. 14;
6. Criminal case No. 102004;
7. Criminal case No. 33028;
8. Criminal case No. 38/33063;
9. Criminal case No. 32053;
10. Criminal case No. 44/33013;
11. Criminal case No. 29187;
12. Criminal case No. 68;
13. Criminal case No. 18/35208 – 91;
14. Criminal case No. 80377/35277;
15. Criminal case No. 80377/64510;
16. Criminal case No. 24634/33020;
17. Criminal case No. 35270;
18. Criminal case No. 39967;
19. Criminal case No. 64516;
20. Criminal case No. 201;
21. Criminal case No. 90013;
22. Criminal case No. 212234;
23. Criminal case No. 208;
24. Criminal case No. 68477;
25. Criminal case No. 69537;
26. Criminal case No. 140.

Literature

1. Criminal Code of the Republic of Azerbaijan (came into force 01.09.2001). Baku – 2013,
2. Criminal Code of the Republic of Azerbaijan (was into force 01.09.2001). Baku – 1995;
3. Nagorno-Karabakh: Chronicle of events. 1988-1994 (based on the official information of Ministry of Internal Affairs (MIA));
4. Нагорный Карабах: События, факты и цифры. Баку – 2005;
5. Rovshan Mustafayev. "Crimes against humankind of Armenian terrorist and bandit formations". Baku – 2002;
6. "Armenian terror". Baku – 2005;
7. Ramiz Mehtiev. "Gorush - 2010 absurd theatre season". Baku – 2010;
8. Vilayat Guliyev. "Armenian atrocities in Azerbaijan". Baku – 2010;
9. Anar Isgenderli. "Realities of Azerbaijan 1917-1920". Baku – 2012;
10. Anar Isgenderli. "Realities of Azerbaijan 1917-1920". US – 2011;
11. Солмаз Рустамова - Тогиди. Азербайджанские погромы в документах. Март 1918 г. Баку – 2009;
12. Azerbaijanis genocide: "Bloody chronicle of history";
13. Эрих Файгл. "Армянская мифомания". Baku – 2007;
14. Erich Feigl. "Armenische Mythomanie". Salzburg – 2007;
15. Джастин Маккарти, Каролин Маккарти. "Тюрки и Армяне". Baku – 1996;
16. J.Mc.Carthy, C. Mc.Carthy. "Turks and Armenians. Amanual on the Armenian Question. Committee on Education Assembly of Turkish American Associations". Washington, D.C. 1989;
17. Samuel A. Uimz. "Secrets of the "Armenian terrorist "Christian" country";

18. Сабир Асадов. "Философия реваншизма или Армянская кровожадность". Baku – 2001;

19. Сабир Асадов, Исрафил Мамедов. "Терроризм причина и следствие". Baku – 2001;

20. "Исторические факты о деяниях армян на Азербайджанской земле". Baku – 2009;

21. Markar Melkonyan. "Road of my brother". New-York – 2005.

Web Resources

1. http://www.human.gov.az
2. http://www.human.gov.az
3. http://www.ermenisorunu.gen.tr/turkce/sorun/isyan7.html
4. http://az.wikipedia.org
5. http://ru.wikipedia.org/wiki
6. http://www.rizvanhuseynov.com
7. http://tr.wikipedia.org/wiki/ASALA
8. http://www.memo.ru/uploads/files/402.pdf
9. http://mfa.gov.az
10. http://d-pankratov.ru
11. http://grani.ru/Events/Disaster/m.226753.htm

Contents

Hertfordshire Press recommended titles

Azerbaijan: Bridge Between East & West
by Yuri Sigov

Azerbaijan is not only a fantastically exotic location on the world map, but also a unique bridge joining Europe and Asia. There has never been a better time to become acquainted with this "emerging energy giant" at the Euro-Asian crossroads. Discover what dreams and hopes this country cherishes and what lies in store for Azerbaijan within the next few years. Alongside this you will realise what an incredible economic, and even more importantly, human potential lies in this amazing and absolutely unusual land.

RRP: £19.50
ISBN: 978-09930444-9-6

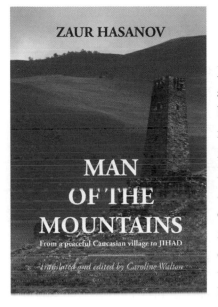

Man of the Mountains
by Zaur Hasanov

Man of the Mountains" is a book about a young Muslim Chechen boy, Zaur who becomes a central figure representing the fight of local indigenous people against both the Russians invading the country and Islamic radicals trying to take a leverage of the situation, using it to push their narrow political agenda on the eve of collapse of the USSR. After 9/11 and the invasion of Iraq and Afghanistan by coalition forces, the subject of the Islamic jihadi movement has become an important subject for the Western readers. But few know about the resistance movement from the local intellectuals and moderates against radical Islamists taking strong hold in the area. "Man of the Mountains" offers a deeper look at the growing influence of Islamic radicals in the Caucasus, particularly in the northern part where the author is from, and its philosophy and operational tools on the ground.

RRP: £14.50
ISBN: 978-09930444-5-8

The Alphabet Game
by Paul Wilson

With the future of Guidebooks under threat, The Alphabet Game takes you back to the very beginning, back to their earliest incarnations and the gamesmanship that brought them into being. As Evelyn Waugh's Scoop did for Foreign Correspondents the world over, so this novel lifts the lid on Travel Writers for good.

Travelling around the world may appear as easy as A,B,C in the twenty first century, but looks can be deceptive: there is no 'X' for a start. Not since Xidakistan was struck from the map. But post 9/11, with the War on Terror going global, the sovereignty of 'The Valley' is back on the agenda. Could the Xidakis, like their Uzbek and Tajik neighbours, be about to taste the freedom of independence? Will Xidakistan once again take its rightful place in the League of Nations?

The Valley's fate is inextricably linked with that of Graham Ruff, founder of Ruff Guides. In a tale setting sail where Around the World in Eighty Days and Lost Horizon weighed anchor, our not-quite-a-hero suffers all the slings and arrows outrageous fortune can muster, in his pursuit of the golden triangle: The Game, The Guidebook, The Girl.

Wilson tells The Game's story with his usual mix of irreverent wit and historical insight, and in doing so delivers the most telling satire on an American war effort since M*A*S*H.

The Guidebook is Dead? Long Live the Guidebook.

RRP: £14.95
ISBN: 978-0-9927873-2-5

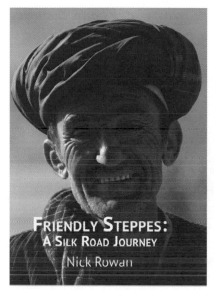

Friendly Steppes:
A Silk Road Journey
by Nick Rowan

This is the chronicle of an extraordinary adventure that led Nick Rowan to some of the world's most incredible and hidden places. Intertwined with the magic of 2,000 years of Silk Road history, he recounts his experiences coupled with a remarkable realisation of just what an impact this trade route has had on our society as we know it today. Containing colourful stories, beautiful photography and vivid characters, and wrapped in the local myths and legends told by the people Nick met and who live along the route, this is both a travelogue and an education of a part of the world that has remained hidden for hundreds of years.

Friendly Steppes: A Silk Road Journey reveals just how rich the region was both culturally and economically and uncovers countless new friends as Nick travels from Venice through Eastern Europe, Iran, the ancient and modern Central Asia of places like Samarkand, Bishkek and Turkmenbashi, and on to China, along the Silk Roads of today.

RRP:£14.95
ISBN: 978-0-9557549-4-4

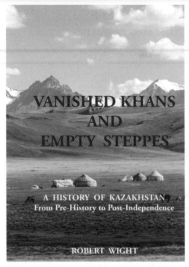

Vanished Khans and Empty Steppes
by Robert Wight

This is a major new history of an increasingly important country in Central Asia.

The book opens with an outline of the history of Almaty, from its nineteenth-century origins as a remote outpost of the Russian empire, up to its present status as the thriving second city of modern-day Kazakhstan. The story then goes back to the Neolithic and early Bronze Ages, and the sensational discovery of the famous Golden Man of the Scythian empire. A succession of armies and empires, tribes and khanates, appeared and disappeared, before the siege and destruction in 1219 of the ancient Silk Road city of Otrar under the Mongol leader Genghis Khan. The emergence of the first identifiable Kazakh state in the sixteenth century was followed by early contacts with Russia, the country which came to be the dominant influence in Kazakhstan and Central Asia for three hundred years. The book shows how Kazakhstan has been inextricably caught up in the vast historical processes – of revolution, civil war, and the rise and fall of communism - which have extended out from Russia over the last century. In the process the country has changed dramatically, from a simple nomadic society of khans and clans, to a modern and outward-looking nation. The transition has been difficult and tumultuous for millions of people, but Vanished Khans and Empty Steppes illustrates how Kazakhstan has emerged as one of the world's most successful post-communist countries.

RRP: £24.50
ISBN: 978-0-9930444-0-3